BEYOND REJECTION

BEYOND REJECTION

The Church, Homosexuality and Hope

DON BAKER

Foreword by Frank Worthen

Portland, Oregon 97266

Cover design by Larry Ulmer
Edited by Liz Heaney

BEYOND REJECTION

Published by Multnomah Press
Portland, Oregon 97266

Printed in the United States of America

Library of Congress Cataloging in Publication Data

Baker, Don.
Beyond rejection.

1. Homosexuality—Religious aspects—Christianity.
I. Title.
BR115.H6B35 1985 261.8'35766 85-8789
ISBN 0-88070-108-0

85 86 87 88 89 90 91 – 10 9 8 7 6 5 4 3 2 1

To the members of
Hinson Memorial Baptist Church
of Portland, Oregon,
without whose forgiveness and acceptance
there would be no story.

Contents

Foreword

"Homosexuals can't change."

It's a lie that has permeated our society. It's accepted as fact within many churches. Most tragic of all, many Christians who struggle with homosexuality have embraced it as reality.

But the heart of the gospel is the hope of new life for all who seek it, including homosexuals. This is the story of one man's victory in embracing that new way of life.

It begins as a story of incredible discouragement and defeat. In my twelve years of ministry to homosexuals, I have met many Christians who struggle in the same silent agony. They have never heard of anyone overcoming homosexuality. They fear they are alone in their battle.

It is the story of a loving wife who never gave up hope. For most homosexuals looking for help, there is a parent or spouse close by who is also in need of ministry and encouragement.

It is the story of friends who gave sacrificially of themselves. This sin problem is not in a special category of its own. Those of us who have labored for years in this field of ministry know that the love of Jesus Christ expressed by concerned Christian friends is one of the most powerful tools of healing.

Most of all, it is the story of one man lifted from a tangled web of sin by the power and grace of God. The lives of Jerry and Rosie continue to be a blessing and an encouragement to those of us who are privileged to know them as friends.

May this book be a beacon of hope to thousands of men and women who have been defeated by homosexuality—but who know in their hearts that Jesus Christ can set them free.

Frank Worthen
Director of Love in Action

CHAPTER ONE

Letters in the Dark

Jerry lay quietly on his bed, watching a light spring rain play softly against the glass of a nearby window.

The house was quiet. Four seminary classmates who shared his living quarters were either asleep or studying for upcoming exams, totally unaware of the destructive drama that was being played out on the stage of Jerry's brain.

A plot was unfolding—the many characters were in place, the curtain was about to rise. The only uncertainty was the audience. Jerry wanted an audience—he needed an audience—for the performance he was planning was to be a "one nighter"—no repeats.

He desperately wanted as many as possible to get the full impact of the message he was about to deliver.

He carefully considered just the right time and just the right place.

There was the Vista Bridge. A graceful old bridge arching itself 112 feet above one of Portland's busiest thoroughfares. Many had used it successfully to make their final statement to a distracted world.

There was the Fremont Bridge—new, high, and beautiful, spanning the swirling, murky waters of the Willamette River. It was just coming into its own as a fairly successful spot to take one's life.

As he thought through these possibilities, he rejected both. Too sudden—too traumatic. Not enough lingering impact to say what he wanted to say. His message had to be given in full view of those who knew him and in such a way that they could never forget the dramatic statement he was about to make.

He chose the place—his bed.

He chose the time—late at night.

He chose the method—a double-edged razor blade to each of his wrists.

Relatively painless, slow, reasonably sure, and terribly messy. A method that would leave his pleading features intact so that his final cry would not go unheard.

He then began composing four letters in his mind. Four strategic letters that had to be written.

The first to his parents.

He wanted desperately to reaffirm his love to them. The last thing Jerry wanted to do was to hurt them. They had wanted to help him but didn't know how.

The problem was too complex—the subject too sensitive. He didn't hold them responsible. But he wanted them to understand. He wanted them to see that he was just too helpless, too hopeless to continue.

The second to the seminary.

He wanted to tell his five hundred classmates and his professors that for nearly three years he had been one of them, and they still didn't know him and didn't care.

Oh, there were some who knew, and there were some who cared, but none of them were able to provide the solution to his nearly life-long problem.

Time and again he would sit through the all-school prayer meetings, trying to muster enough courage to raise his hand and ask for prayer. Most of the time was spent talking about prayer rather than praying. When the opportunity was finally given, invariably the leader would close with some remark like "Now be specific, feel free to share what's really on your heart, but remember, this is not the time or the place to hang out our dirty laundry—that should be done in private."

Jerry would then settle back in his seat, heave a frustrated sigh, and wrap what he considered was his "dirty laundry" tightly about himself and eventually leave with the same heavy

burden with which he had come.

Another letter was to be addressed to the editor of the Portland *Oregonian*.

He wanted someone to publish the fact that there were homosexuals in Portland who really wanted to change. There was at least one who could not march or carry a banner in a gay pride parade.

There was one, at least, who was frightened and even ashamed of the reputation his city was getting. Portland was fast gaining the distinction of being "the gay Mecca," or "another San Francisco." It was acquiring names like The Homosexual Haven and The Camp and even Boys Town because of the ever-increasing number of young male prostitutes who regularly presented themselves for hire on the streets of downtown Portland.

If only he could tell his city that there were some gays who were struggling to get out of their subculture.

His last letter was to be written to his roommates.

To them he would say: "I have lived with you, prayed with you, studied with you, laughed with you—even cried with you, but none of you ever sensed where and how I was really struggling. I can't blame you and I don't. I was afraid to tell you. I feared your rejection more than anything else in the world. I really don't hold you responsible—but I do wish you had been able to help me."

Jerry composed and recomposed his final messages—messages that had been inspired by a week-long string of devastating events that had finally culminated with his exposure as a homosexual and his withdrawal from seminary.

Jerry hurt as he had never hurt before in his entire life, but he did not fear death—even the haunting and ugly form of death he had chosen.

Jerry's greatest fear was life—a life that had become far more frustrating and painful than he could any longer endure.

CHAPTER TWO

Obsession

The levels of guilt and despair had been building for years.

Jerry had long since learned that biblical Christianity and homosexuality, like all forms of sexual sin, are mutually incompatible. They simply cannot happily exist in the same person at the same time.

Jerry had entered both lives as a child. He had accepted God's love and forgiveness at age six and had experienced his first homosexual encounter just three years later.

His life as a gay began in his backyard in a pup tent with a neighbor boy of about the same age.

As they lay side by side on the ground, they would fondle one another's bodies, first with curiosity, then with fear followed by guilt.

Later Jerry began having very positive feelings about his childhood adventure. For what may have been the first time in all his young life, he had the strong feeling that somebody really liked him. Being liked and genuinely accepted was a strange and elusive feeling that Jerry had seldom experienced before.

Then Jerry's friend moved to another city. Their encounters were put to an end, except for once when the families visited. On this occasion Jerry's mother walked into the room where the two were fondling each other. The level of shock and embarrassment

was so great that she actually excused herself and backed out the door, not knowing what to do or to say.

Jerry spent much of his time in junior high school fantasizing about other fellow's bodies.

His activity was limited in high school, but he was always aware that the consuming desire of his thought life was to see a guy in the nude.

His concentration was constantly being broken in church or in school by fantasies that usually involved a physical relationship with a popular, masculine, athletic man with a firm, lean, attractive body. Jerry never viewed himself as any of these, but he was always searching for the ideal man who would become the ultimate sex partner and provide those feelings of love and acceptance he so deeply craved.

During his four years of college and an additional four years in the military, he became increasingly aware of other men with similar feelings and similar needs. He began seeking out regular encounters. Oftentimes he'd wait in public restrooms; sometimes he would find someone there already waiting. These encounters were usually brief but would eventually result in some homosexual act.

For Jerry there would be short periods of abstinence followed by successive days and nights of feverish sexual activity. At times it seemed cyclical, at other times it was continuous.

Jerry's homosexual experiences reached a peak while he was preparing for Christian ministry in seminary. The intense academic pressure with the increased spiritual pressure seemed to trigger an even greater and more obsessive need for sexual release.

He would spend his days in the seminary classrooms and his nights "cruising" the streets of Portland.

A confirmed, practicing homosexual, he would walk into any one of the city's many gay bars, sit down at one of the tables, order a glass of beer, and begin "looking over the merchandise."

"The merchandise" always took the form of the bodies and faces of dozens of quiet, clean, well-groomed men of all ages—most in their twenties and thirties.

In the early evening a gay bar appears like any other favorite meeting place for young people. As the evening wears on, however, many of the men find a male partner, pair off, talk, drink, or

dance together to the ever-present beat of the music.

Some of the many faces Jerry peered into would look expectant, some distracted. Some appeared lonely, but most were looking for that special someone who could give them some semblance of physical satisfaction.

Jerry would look through the cigarette haze that shrouded the dimly lighted room until he found just the right partner. The two would then talk, drink, and often dance until they would eventually move out to the car or some other private place where they would mutually satisfy each other's insistent sexual desires.

At times Jerry would leave the bars so drunk that when he awakened the next morning in a stranger's car or a stranger's house, he was unaware of where he was and what he had done. He would have no memory of what had taken place the night before.

Often Jerry would park his car on a distant side street and move furtively to Portland's popular gay bath where hundreds of homosexuals would meet each night for sexual activity. He would hide his wallet under the seat of the car, remove all other forms of personal identification, take out just enough money to get beyond the guarded door, and then quickly enter the old four-story hotel that offered nearly every form of homosexual activity a man might desire.

He would remove his clothes, wrap himself in a towel, and move from room to room, looking for that perfect partner and that ultimate experience.

In all of his years of searching for both, however, he found neither.

The constant guilt was unbearable. He felt guilt as he would anticipate an encounter; he felt guilt during an encounter; he felt unendurable guilt following an encounter.

As his level of homosexual activity increased, there was a corresponding increase in his level of guilt.

He prayed constantly for deliverance. At times he would direct his anger away from himself and aim it straight at God for not answering his prayer.

He found it difficult to understand how "the God of the impossible" did not seem able to transform his life.

He often hoped that someone would lovingly confront him, offer help, and even demand a relationship of accountability.

He even wished for someone to discover his problem, uncover his sin, and expose him as a homosexual so that his charade would be brought to an end.

But it never happened.

God did not transform him.

No one ever confronted him.

No one ever exposed him as a homosexual.

Many times, over a period of more than twenty years, he would emit a small plea for help. His cries were usually heard by someone who either didn't understand . . . or didn't care.

He talked to his mother. She was concerned but uncomfortable with the subject.

He could never discuss his problem with his father.

He talked to his family doctor without fully revealing his problem. He was given some basic information on sex and a booklet describing the facts of life.

While in Germany he consulted an army psychiatrist who advised him to begin having some sexual experiences with female prostitutes. "In time," he said, "you'll lose your interest in men."

His attempts to get discharged from the army were frustrated by a ruling which required that he actually be "caught in the act" and by fear of the stigma of a dishonorable discharge.

A Campus Crusade staff member told him, "It's just a passing thing—stay in the Scriptures and pray and you'll be all right."

He shared his burden with his aunt, with an army buddy, and with a roommate. Each expressed genuine concern and promised to pray for him, but no one offered answers.

A psychologist spent nearly three months with Jerry, trying to help build his self-esteem.

He told two well-known Christian leaders, but only so much. All he could tell them was that he had a "besetting sin" and desperately needed prayer. Neither of them probed beyond his request. He wished they had.

At the time he was seriously considering suicide, I had been his pastor only four months. He did not tell me.

It has always been of great concern to me that he never felt that freedom. I've often wondered, if he had, would I have been any more confrontive than the others? Would I have been accepting? Would I have had any solutions or even any suggestions?

Or would I, like so many others, have been so repulsed that I would have completely rejected a Christian brother who was desperately seeking help?

I must confess, I probably would have been unable to help, and possibly even unwilling.

CHAPTER THREE

Out of the Closet

Jerry's third year in seminary was his crisis year. His high grades were slipping. His level of concentration was shorter. His guilt was fast becoming unbearable.

He made an appointment with one of his professors to ask what he needed to do in this third year of classes to bolster his sagging grades.

He nervously paced the carpeted hallway outside his professor's office.

He seriously considered canceling the appointment.

Finally the door opened and in his characteristicly fidgety fashion, Jerry moved in, sat down, and began to talk.

It is always somewhat difficult to counsel with Jerry. He is bilingual and articulate, but he seldom, if ever, ends a sentence. His thoughts run together and constantly trigger new thoughts that make it hard to understand what he is really trying to say.

From the time he begins his verbal trip until he reaches his destination, he usually manages to take so many detours that one has to listen long and intently to understand why he has come.

This time was no different.

He kept looking furtively about the room, nervously moving his hands up and down and back and forth. He repeatedly punctuated his long and disjointed monologue with deep and heavy sighs.

His professor listened patiently.

When Jerry finished, this rather austere-looking but compassionate and godly man began thumbing through his grade book. He confirmed that there was a definite and serious decline in his student's grades.

He then asked Jerry about his other classes.

With difficulty Jerry began to admit he was having trouble with all of his subjects.

The professor looked up from his desk and into the troubled eyes of his young friend for a long time. His intense gaze, though softened by his ever-present love and concern, seemed to bore into Jerry's soul.

The good doctor was searching—thinking—praying—wondering.

Finally, with characteristic wisdom, he asked, "Jerry, is there anything else that's bothering you in your life right now?"

He waited.

Jerry squirmed, bowed his head, began to shrink into his chair, and paled perceptibly. Beads of perspiration suddenly appeared on his forehead.

After what seemed like hours of ominous, interminable silence, Jerry sat bolt upright, took a deep breath, heaved a long sigh, and said, "Yes, there is something."

Before Jerry could go any further, the professor held up his hand and said, "Jerry, stop right there. I sense that whatever is bothering you is something very deep. I don't wish to pry—and I certainly don't want you to tell me if you really don't want to—but if you'd like to share it with me, feel free to go ahead. I may not be able to help, but I'll try—and you can be assured that I will keep whatever you say in the strictest confidence."

Jerry waited a long time before he continued. "This isn't easy for me to tell you, but I've been struggling with homosexuality for most of my life."

He paused and waited for a reaction. He fully expected rejection.

There was none.

In its place was compassion, a deep sense of pain, and an unexpected feeling of complete acceptance.

He then proceeded to relate his struggle and concluded by stating that he was a closet homosexual, leading a double life and unable to continue.

"Have you ever sought counseling?"

"I've had some, but none that was long-term."

"Do you think it might be helpful?"

"I really don't know."

The professor sat quietly for a long time and then said, "Jerry, I have a problem that I must acknowledge to you. I stated earlier that you could feel free to tell me anything and that you could be assured of my complete confidence. It won't be long before you will be ready to graduate from Western Seminary. A degree from Western not only means you have satisfactorily completed all the assigned requirements for graduation, but it also means that the faculty and staff of Western are convinced that you are fully qualified morally and spiritually as well as academically to serve God wherever God may choose to place you.

"Do you realize, Jerry," he continued, "that prior to commencement I'll be asked to sit in a faculty meeting and review the names of every candidate for a degree from this institution? I'll be asked if I know of any reason why you as a member of the graduating class should not be awarded your degree. At that time I'll be obliged to honor my responsibility to this institution and the churches we serve. It may be necessary for me to break this confidence and tell my peers about your struggle with homosexuality.

"Do I have your permission to do that?"

There was a long silence as Jerry sat motionless, stunned, gradually becoming aware of the implications of his unexpected confession.

Slowly, soberly, he asked, "Do you think I should withdraw from school?"

"I don't know what you should do, Jerry. It's really not for me to decide. The only thing I can suggest is that we both go home, pray, and seek God's wisdom in the matter and meet together in my office on Monday."

Jerry left feeling exposed and aware that his seminary days were over and his life-long dream of Christian ministry had come to an abrupt end.

The following Monday both he and the professor agreed that any decision regarding Jerry's future rested with the administration. Jerry agreed to go himself and tell his story.

The seminary's vice-president listened with the same compassion, displayed the same acceptance, but shared all the same

concerns previously expressed by the professor. He suggested, however, that the severity of Jerry's problem really required the attention of the president.

Dr. Earl Radmacher was the last person with whom Jerry wanted to talk about his struggle with homosexuality. The president had asked Jerry to join him while ministering in Europe. Jerry was scheduled to interpret his messages in to German.

As much as Jerry loved and respected Dr. Radmacher, he also feared him. He had always regarded him as scholarly, firm, distant—even unapproachable.

Jerry thought that the president's response would include not only a sense of great personal disappointment but also a severe reprimand and quick expulsion from the seminary.

As Jerry talked, he became aware of two brown eyes that soon filled with tears as his deep hurt was being transferred to the caring heart of the seminary president.

Jerry found himself willing to submit to any decision in the presence of such compassion.

Dr. Radmacher said, "Jerry, I really don't know much about homosexuality. I've counseled with two, maybe three people, and I'm not really sure that I helped them. I don't know how to counsel you or even what books to recommend. I do feel you need some competent professional counseling, though. And Jerry, I do think you should withdraw from seminary until your life is under control and you've had time to prove that you're qualified to serve Christ."

Jerry agreed. He knew there were no other options.

He realized that the decision was both compassionate and correct. But it was wrenching.

His world had collapsed.

His future was in doubt.

His past was fully exposed.

The days that followed were a blur. He was unaware of anything but an overwhelming sense of futility.

Now as he lay on his bed, calculating his suicide and mentally composing his four final letters, something totally unexpected happened.

God intervened.

Without warning Jerry fell into exhausted sleep.

When he awakened the next morning, he was stunned that

he was still alive. Stunned, but reluctantly thankful.

He slipped out from under the covers, placed his feet on the cold, bare floor, and began to walk tentatively into a new day, a new life, a whole new world. A world filled with uncertainty, but possibly a world that included some small thread of hope: the hope that—just maybe—his life could change.

"But no, that's impossible," he thought.

To change from being a homosexual was more than he dared hope. It was even more than he dared pray.

He was convinced that homosexuals were permanently trapped in a life style they either were forced to accept, or what seemed even worse to him, forced to struggle with as long as they lived.

"Homosexuals never change . . . they can't change," he thought, and he had had more than twenty years of experience to confirm that painful conclusion.

CHAPTER FOUR

"Is It Possible to Change?"

Out of seminary, out of money, and desperately low on self-esteem, Jerry went out to seek employment.

He found work as a teamster—a full-time job loading and unloading trucks on the docks.

His small body, noticeably lacking the muscular strength characteristic of most dock-workers, made his work extremely difficult. After a ten-to-twelve-hour shift, he would drive home exhausted.

His job required no intellectual challenge—no academic stimulation. He was bored.

But the pay was good. And the spiritual pressure of seminary was off. He was free in every way to do as he pleased—when and where he pleased and for as long as he pleased. For a brief time he felt a freedom to engage in any and every homosexual activity.

In Jerry's alone moments, however, the guilt came back with unyielding intensity. Life seemed empty, burned over, like the cold ashes of a long-dead fire.

It wasn't long before he decided to look for that competent, professional counseling that had been recommended by so many.

Nearly three months passed from the time of his first phone call to the time of his first appointment. These agonizing months

could have been shortened considerably if he had been willing to discuss the severity of his problem with the counselor's secretary, but he could not. Too many people already knew. Even the prospect of sharing it with a counselor seemed both frightening and futile.

When he was finally seated across from the counselor, he found himself uncomfortable.

The doctor's greeting had been warm and friendly. His demeanor was cordial and nonthreatening, but when he asked Jerry, "What would you like to talk about today?" Jerry's immediate impulse was to bolt out of the room and run as far away as possible.

He chose to stay.

As he sat there, thinking of a response, he studied his counselor carefully.

His first observations were physical—as always with men.

This man was overweight, considerably older, and sexually unattractive. Jerry was relieved. At least his counselor was not a threat to him in his area of greatest weakness.

Finally Jerry answered. "I'd like to talk to you about the biggest struggle of my life."

"And what's that, Jerry?"

Jerry evaded this directness by saying, "The reason I've chosen you as a counselor is that you have been highly recommended by my seminary professors."

He paused. The counselor was silent.

"I'm desperate for help," Jerry pleaded.

The silence continued.

Jerry sighed again and said, "No one seems to have any answer to my problem."

Silence.

"I've asked many people to help me, but they were unable."

Silence.

Nervously, Jerry blurted out his most agonizing confession one more time: "I'm a practicing homosexual."

Jerry searched the counselor's face. He looked for signs of surprise, rejection, discomfort. There were none.

He had hoped for some sign of loving compassion—tenderness, tears, gentleness—but these were also absent.

There was no surprise or shock. There was no indication of

revulsion or shame. Just "Oh. Do you think I can be of help?"

"Have you ever counseled a homosexual?"

"Yes, I have counseled some, but not many."

Jerry felt immediate disappointment. "Oh no," he thought, "not another inexperienced novice." But Jerry had already waited three months and was out twenty-five dollars for this appointment. He decided to continue.

The counselor spent considerable time making his client comfortable, all the while very much aware of the fidgety desperation written all over the face of this young man.

He noticed his embarrassment. He observed his guilt. He watched the shame and frustration etched on his features. He wanted to help, but he knew how great were the odds against permanent or even long-term change in the life style of a homosexual.

He prayed for wisdom.

Jerry broke the silence with a pleading question—a question to which he felt he already knew the answer—a question that had been answered by his devastating, depressing inability to bring his body under control. A question answered time and time again by the shout of the overwhelming power of habit. Yet he asked his question one more time.

"Do you believe that it's possible for a homosexual to change?"

"Yes, I believe you can change if you really want to. I can't change you. It won't be easy—in fact, it will be extremely difficult, but I believe you can change."

"How long will it take?"

"Probably a long time."

"A year?"

"Probably at least a year."

"Longer?"

"Quite possibly it could take longer."

"There is no instant cure for homosexuality," the counselor went on to explain. "There have been many who have claimed instant deliverance and possibly some have experienced it, but most of those who make such claims tend to slip silently back into their old habit patterns."

Jerry had hoped for a little more optimism and a lot less time, but in spite of his disappointment, he set up dates for

regularly scheduled appointments with his new friend.

As he left the counselor's office, Jerry felt a great need for love. He needed a man. He needed another encounter.

He argued with himself for the rest of that day. He had taken his first big step. He was finally on his way to becoming straight. He couldn't go back now.

And he didn't—for two whole days.

CHAPTER FIVE

One Small Step

During the months of counseling that followed, Jerry slowly unfolded the story of his life.

He recalled that by age three he was well aware that when he was born his mother had wanted a daughter instead of a son. Occasionally he overheard his parents refer to this, and he began to feel that he had been a disappointment to them.

As he reflected on his childhood, he recalled that he seemed to be far more concerned about pleasing his mother than his father. His father and brother shared an interest in hunting and fishing. Jerry's father would often invite him to go with them on their hunting and fishing trips. Occasionally Jerry would go on a fishing trip, but it soon became obvious that this was not his real interest. He couldn't stand the sight of worms or the feel of the fish, and the criticism he received was unbearable.

The unhappy excursions often ended with feelings of guilt and shame, and he would return home feeling more isolated than ever from his father.

He drifted toward his mother and her interests and began developing feminine characteristics. He spent much of his time cleaning house, cooking, washing dishes, and doing household chores. He learned to knit and to bake. By the time he was in junior high school he was sometimes doing his mother's hair.

As he reviewed his early years, Jerry recalled that his first grade teacher had penned a note on his report card which read, "Jerry needs to learn to play with the boys more and not to play with the girls so much."

At the end of that same year another note was sent from school. "I would continue to urge you to encourage Jerry to become active in athletics and sports and not to play with the girls so much."

Jerry developed a love for music and books. He learned to play the piano, organ, accordian, alto saxophone, and trumpet.

He became actively involved in church and developed strong relationships with Christians. His desire to be a missionary became compelling.

Then he met his neighbor.

Jerry went on with his story week after week. He explained how his homosexuality had begun and how it had progressed to the point where he was asked to give up his lifelong dream and leave seminary.

The counseling began to pay off. Within four weeks of his first session, his encounters began to diminish, and not long after Jerry stopped them altogether.

He couldn't pinpoint any one reason for his new-found control. He was spending more time in the Scriptures. He had gone through the major crisis of exposure and seminary withdrawal and survived. And he was paying twenty-five dollars a visit. This last fact was possibly more instrumental than he wanted to admit.

And then there was Dan Britts.

Dan and Jerry had met in seminary. They lived in the same dorm and attended the same classes.

Jerry's first reaction to Dan when he saw him seated in the large lecture hall was, "Man, that's a good-looking guy."

Jerry admired Dan and envied him for his good looks, his popularity, and his discipline. Dan was athletic and jogged daily. It wasn't long before Jerry was jogging with him, eating and studying with him, and spending most of his time with his new friend.

When Jerry finally confessed to Dan that he was a practicing homosexual, Dan's eyes immediately filled with tears. Jerry's pain had been transmitted to a caring brother.

Although he knew nothing about homosexuality, Dan was willing to learn enough to be of help.

Dan made a commitment to Jerry that was never broken. "Jerry, I want you to feel free to call me or come and talk with me at any time—day or night. I will always be available to you."

That commitment was put to the test countless times.

Often Jerry would call in the middle of the night and say, "Dan, I've just done it again."

Dan's response was always the same: "Would you like to come over and talk about it, Jerry?"

"But Dan, it's the middle of the night."

"That's OK. I'll fix us a cup of coffee to help us stay awake so we can talk."

The first year in seminary Dan was single, but even after his marriage that commitment never wavered. Jerry was always welcome.

Jerry would arrive at Dan's and they would take their coffee to the little study in the basement.

For a few brief moments they would sit in silence and then look at each other. Both would start to cry.

Together they would look up Scripture, and Dan would always ask, "Jerry, do you acknowledge that what you have done tonight is sin?"

"Yes," Jerry would answer. He had never, since age nine, condoned or excused his actions. They were always sinful.

Dan would then ask if he had asked God's forgiveness.

Jerry's answer was always the same. "Oh yes, again and again—so many times that I'm ashamed to keep going back to him. How can he keep on forgiving me? How can he keep on loving me? Dan, do you think I'm really a Christian? Can I be a Christian and keep on sinning like this?"

Patiently, lovingly, Dan would review the same basic Scriptures each time that question was asked.

John 3:16, John 3:18, Romans 5:8, 1 John 5:11 and 12, Ephesians 2:8 and 9—Scriptures designed to build up Jerry's faith and remind him that his salvation was dependent upon what Jesus Christ had done with sin on the cross of Calvary, not upon what Jerry himself had done.

Dan would remind Jerry that he was a child of God, that

Jerry had rejected himself—he had not rejected God, and God had certainly not rejected him.

This little scenario was repeated dozens of times, with no lessening of the temptation on Jerry's part and no evidence of impatience from Dan.

Many times Dan would say, "Jerry, why don't you try calling me before you go downtown instead of afterwards?"

Jerry never did—until about the fourth week into his counseling.

He left home one Saturday night about 10:30 and started for his favorite gay bar. There was no indication of a struggle. But on the way God gently reminded him of his friend.

Stopping at a phone booth, Jerry dropped in a coin, dialed, and impatiently waited for Dan to answer. He was convinced that the call would be of no help whatsoever, but he did want to honor Dan's request.

"Dan, I'm calling as you requested—and believe it or not, it's before the fact. I'm planning to go downtown and to get involved with someone—what do you want to tell me?"

"Well, Jerry, I think you just ought to turn around and go back home to bed," Dan answered.

Jerry laughed and told him how ridiculous that sounded. "It's just not that easy."

Dan persisted. "Tell me, Jerry, just why do you want to go downtown?"

"I'm feeling strongly tempted and lonely. I just don't want to fight it—I'm tired of the battle."

Jerry tried desperately to get Dan off the phone. Finally, with a voice filled with exasperation, Jerry shouted, "Go ahead and finish telling me what you want to tell me, because I've got to get going."

Jerry knew that Dan and Sue were entertaining friends and was convinced that Dan would soon give up on him.

But he didn't.

"I'm not going to hang up, Jerry."

"But Dan, you can't do that to me. It's not fair."

"Jerry, let's pray."

"I can't pray—I don't want to pray."

"Will you let me pray for you, Jerry?"

"OK—go ahead." Jerry realized that his arguments were useless.

Dan started praying, and God began melting Jerry's heart.

When Dan had finished, he again asked, "Now, Jerry, will you go home?"

"I wish it were that easy," Jerry said softly. "I wish I could go home. I wish I could assure you that I'd go home—but I can't."

One more time Dan asked gently but firmly, "Jerry, will you go home and go to bed?"

There was a long silence—followed by a heavy sigh and a quiet but firm, "Yes."

Jerry went home and to bed.

For the first time in his long career as a practicing homosexual, he had finally broken the power of that compelling temptation.

He had taken just one small step.

He had obeyed God, and when he did, God calmed his wild, uncontrollable sex drive, and he went to bed and slept—a deep, peaceful sleep.

CHAPTER SIX

Jerry Tells Rosie

Then Jerry fell in love.

Jerry and Rosie had just driven home from a delightful evening together. As they sat and talked outside Rosie's apartment, Jerry grew increasingly quiet.

Their relationship had been developing over the past six months to the point where each was thinking separately of engagement and marriage, though neither had mentioned it.

Finally Jerry gave Rosie's hand an extra firm squeeze, nervously shifted his feet on the floor of the 1968 V.W. bug, and said, "Rosie, I have something very important that I need to talk to you about."

"Go ahead," she said, never once imagining the enormity of the bomb that was about to be dropped on her unsuspecting world.

"You know I've been getting counseling during these last few months—sometimes it has even interfered with our dating schedule. Have you ever wondered why I was being counseled?"

"Oh, I've thought about it. But I'm not really curious to know at this point."

Jerry gave another quick sigh and said, "I have a sexual orientation problem."

Rosie was silent but quick to mentally sift through a number

of possibilities. "Perhaps Jerry doesn't like sex . . . perhaps he has a sexual dysfunction . . . perhaps he just doesn't feel sexual toward women, or . . . perhaps he doesn't feel sexual toward me." The thought never occurred to her that Jerry just might be a homosexual.

"Let's go upstairs and talk about this," Rosie said.

She felt honored Jerry would talk to her about something this important. All the way up the stairs both were silent.

Jerry was holding Rosie's hand. Surprisingly, she felt calm and in control. "He had a pretty jumpy hand," Rosie remembers. "In fact, Jerry was very nervous. He was really messing my hand up. I was surprised when we finally reached my door and I still had five fingers left."

Rosie asked Jerry, "What do you mean you have a sexual orientation problem?"

"I have been struggling with homosexuality all of my life," Jerry finally answered. "That's why I'm seeking counsel."

During the brief silence that followed Jerry was sure that this was the end—the end of a relationship that was filled with delightful promise. Rosie would suggest that they should stop dating, or worse, she would even break the friendship. The only thing Jerry could hope to recover from his admission was that they maintain some sort of distant friendship that would allow for at least limited communication between them, but even that possibility seemed remote.

"What do you think of me now?" Jerry asked. "Do you think any less of me?" "Oh no, Jerry," Rosie answered. "I do not think less of you. I think more highly of you because you have trusted me so much that you have shared your greatest problem with me—voluntarily."

As they sat on the living room couch in Rosie's modest but decorative apartment, they held hands with no feeling of discomfort while Jerry recounted his life story. It was somewhat abbreviated. There were some things he could tell his counselor that he just couldn't tell Rosie.

Rosie was very encouraged. Jerry had been celibate now for nearly five months, and that just had to mean that this wonderful man's problem was a thing of the past—and then, even if it wasn't, she was sure she could satisfy any and all needs that might still have been left over from Jerry's past.

Rosie reminded Jerry of her deep love for him and expressed her appreciation for his honesty.

They kissed good night, and he left.

Already they were beginning to feel like a team. They were both convinced that with the commitment they felt toward each other, they would and could see this thing through.

After Jerry left, Rosie reflected deeply on the entire evening's discussion.

Gays were not strangers to her. She worked with some and had begun seeing them as people with needs just like everyone else.

But Jerry was different. He was a homosexual who had been cured. Five months of celibacy had proved that, hadn't it?

How she loved Jerry. It was the greatest, most consuming love she had ever known. Until they met, she was convinced that she would remain a contented single, but now she realized just how much she wanted the right man to come along—and Jerry was just that man, so totally committed to God. God was always present in their relationship. They often prayed together and read their Bibles together.

She felt no apprehension over his confession. She was certain the problem would never come up again.

It was seldom ever discussed.

Occasionally she would ask Jerry how the counseling sessions were going, and once or twice she did ask him, more out of curiosity than anything, whether or not he was still celibate.

Rosie did no research whatsoever on the subject of homosexuality.

Four months later, Jerry proposed.

It was Mother's Day, 1975. They were on top of beautiful Mt. Tabor, just a short distance from Western Seminary, both feeling guilty for not being with their mothers.

Rosie remembers that Jerry was especially nervous that day—he was again milking her hand with his, obviously trying to muster enough courage to say something of great significance to him.

Finally Jerry sighed, reached into his pocket, and pulled out a carefully prepared document listing twenty-five reasons why he loved Rosie, and then proceeded to say, "Rosie, I love you very much. Would you be my wife?"

Rosie remembers being completely shocked, but quickly answered, "Yes, I will."

I had encouraged them to get married. Without ever mentioning the homosexuality problem, they had come to me to seek counsel on dating and to learn some guidelines to use in preparing for engagement.

I remember being impressed with the fact that they were not asking me to marry them—they were asking how I felt about their getting married. It's so seldom I am ever privileged to be a part of that decision-making process. I encouraged them, at their ages, to plan on a short engagement, marry soon, and marry each other. I was convinced they were perfectly suited for one another.

My wife encouraged them. When she heard the news, Martha excitedly told Jerry that she had been wondering when he was going to get around to asking Rosie.

Everyone was excited over Jerry and Rosie's engagement—everyone except his counselor. When Jerry told him that he had proposed, the counselor began to express many reservations.

"Jerry, you need a longer period of celibacy before marriage. You need to develop a whole new sexual orientation—you need to develop an entirely new thought life. I'm not sure that you've given this important project the time it needs, Jerry."

Jerry had a deep respect for his counselor, but his reservations and fears were filed away for future reference. Jerry did not doubt that he would be sexually compatible with Rosie. He listened carefully to the suggestions to wait, to postpone—and then ignored them.

They counseled with me three times prior to their wedding. Our relationship was one of those that made me glad I was a pastor. I loved them dearly, was honored with the privilege of officiating at their wedding, and entered into their plans and dreams with great excitement and expectancy.

I asked them all the usual questions and then told them, "I'm going to ask you four questions. I don't want a quick response. Take them home with you—think them over—don't discuss them between yourselves, and then bring your answers back next week."

We reviewed both the questions and the answers a few days later.

"Jerry, what do you love most about Rosie?"

"She's a good listener."

"Rosie, what do you love most about Jerry?"

"Jerry is a godly man, and I'm attracted to his spiritual maturity. He constantly challenges me."

"Jerry, what is the one thing about Rosie that irritates you?"

At this point Jerry hesitated, flushed, and finally answered, "Her weight problem." Rosie was heavy—always had been. She wanted to lose at least fifty pounds before the wedding, but never came close.

"Rosie, what is the one thing about Jerry that irritates you?"

"His indecisiveness. He has such a hard time making decisions."

They both laughed at each other's responses, agreed to their reality, and then proceeded to plan the ceremony.

The subject of homosexuality was never introduced.

Both sets of parents gave their approval.

The church family was excited.

The wedding, with nearly four hundred in attendance, was everything Jerry and Rosie had ever dreamed.

The wedding night exceeded their expectations. The intimacies they shared gave them both sheer joy and delight. They agreed that it had been worth waiting for.

Their first three months of marriage had its normal periods of adjustment, but they were delightful months, filled with contentment and joy.

Then just ninety-one days after one of Hinson's most beautiful weddings—without warning and without apparent reason—Jerry left his office, headed downtown, sought out his favorite gay bar, and then left it with a total male stranger to again have sex in a dimly lighted downtown public restroom.

CHAPTER SEVEN

"What's It Going to Take?"

For two days Jerry was distant, irritable, restless, and evasive.

In desperation he analyzed that unexpected but unforgettable homosexual encounter.

Why? Why? Why?

There had been the year of effective counsel.

There had been that momentous decision prompted by his friend Dan.

There had been over a year of celibacy.

There had been three months of marriage.

There had been significant spiritual growth.

Why had he fallen again?

Some possible reasons surfaced.

There were growing feelings of unhappiness, frustration, and inadequacy.

He was selling insurance on straight commission, and things were not going well. His best month had netted him only $900.

Rosie's $469 per month didn't help their income all that much.

Their sexual adjustment was far more difficult than he had expected. Memories of homosexual encounters would creep into

his mind while he and Rosie were making love.

He found himself comparing Rosie to some of the men he had known and constantly asking himself the question, "Which is better, a man or a woman?"

His thought life was out of control. His mind kept probing in directions he did not want to go, but he felt helpless to redirect it.

He was failing as a husband, haunted by his inability to give spiritual leadership to Rosie.

The level of commitment in marriage seemed far more than he had bargained for.

Then there was Rosie's weight. Jerry was very much aware of her appearance and began harassing her as she ate.

Rosie had no clue as to what was happening. She was convinced that Jerry's life as a homosexual was in the past.

She worried about his detachment, but thought it was due to another day of poor sales.

Finally he could contain the truth no longer.

Jerry snuggled close, feeling ashamed and embarrassed. He began to sob convulsively.

"Oh Rosie, Rosie, I'm so sorry. I don't know how to tell you this, and it's not going to be easy. I must tell you, though. I want to tell you. Rosie, I've fallen again.

"Two nights ago I was at the office. I was feeling under strong temptation, and the old memories started surfacing, and I just couldn't fight it any longer. I wrestled in my mind whether or not to give in and then realized it was hopeless. I went downtown," and again Jerry began to sob, "and . . . and . . . I met a stranger, and we had sex together."

Rosie stiffened and was silent.

"For the last two days," Jerry said, "I've been in terrible turmoil. I just had to tell you."

Jerry's whole body shook as he sobbed out the details to his wife.

"Oh, I wish I hadn't gone," he continued. "Oh, how I hate myself. I just can't continue to live without asking forgiveness. I've not only sinned against God, but I've sinned against you. I want to ask your forgiveness for what I did two nights ago."

Rosie went numb. She was totally confused.

She listened to the words. She felt the heaving sobs in her

husband's body. She heard her husband's plea. She saw the deep pain in his eyes.

How could this happen in their beautiful marriage? It was like opening the door to a dark tomb that had been sealed shut. Suddenly there was nothing but ugliness.

Fear consumed her.

What does this do to the oneness we have been enjoying and building?

What is this powerful hand that has risen to smash us?

Those thoughts were quickly forgotten as her concern for Jerry took charge. He was devastated . . . broken.

She drew Jerry close and held him until the sobs began to subside.

"Oh Jerry, I do forgive you. I just ache with you. You must be hurting badly."

She wiped the tears from his face, and she felt his whole body relax as her words swept over him.

Jerry was overwhelmed with relief. He was surprised that forgiveness could be so prompt—so complete.

To Jerry it seemed that Rosie was confirmation of God's forgiveness.

She had every right to be angry—to threaten—to leave. Without even thinking it over she had forgiven him.

Jerry spontaneously began to pray: "Father, I thank you for Rosie's love for me and for enabling her to forgive me totally. I claim your promise of forgiveness in 1 John 1:9, but I find it so hard to forgive myself. I don't know what it will take to get these thoughts out of my mind, but I ask you again to take them from me and to give me strength to obey you. Please give Rosie and me the grace to fight this battle.

"I know you brought us together—we married by design, not by chance, and Father, I know you are not going to leave us orphaned."

Jerry stopped. His whole body trembled before he could continue. He heaved a great sigh and said, "Father, I pray that you will heal all the pain and all the hurt that I've caused Rosie."

Rosie couldn't pray.

They fell asleep in each other's arms, at peace with God and with each other.

Jerry was convinced that his homosexuality was in the past,

Rosie was relaxed with the assurance that this one-timer would never be repeated.

Both were mistaken. Within weeks Jerry found himself again yielding to the overpowering urges that had controlled his life for so long.

CHAPTER EIGHT

Devastation

As Jerry's encounters continued and increased in frequency, Rosie's world collapsed.

At first Jerry confessed; later he lapsed into silence.

Rosie began to despise the emotional instability she saw. Each time she would question Jerry to determine some reason for his behavior, but many times he refused to respond.

"Do you realize what you're doing to our marriage? Do you know what this is doing to the oneness we so enjoyed?"

"I don't want to talk about it—just don't ask me any questions," Jerry would say as he would go into his study, close the door, and barricade himself from his wife.

Rosie would stand in the hallway looking at the closed door, wondering what was happening to them.

Would they be able to see this through?

Was victory possible, especially now with Jerry's increased involvement?

What had happened? Hadn't he been cured?

"I know we're having difficulty adjusting to this marriage, but is that sufficient explanation for his behavior?" she thought.

Rosie began to wonder if she was making impossible emotional demands on Jerry.

Was she clinging too tightly?

Was she smothering him or mothering him?

She constantly feared the possibility that he might come home with a disease.

She wondered if they were both going to be destroyed by homosexuality.

Jerry insisted on complete confidentiality. He refused Rosie permission to talk to anyone. He lived in constant fear of exposure. His job, his reputation, his very life was at stake, he said.

Late one night after a severe argument, Rosie decided she could no longer bear the pain alone. She called a close friend.

As soon as Rosie heard her friend's voice, she began to sob. Marilyn waited patiently. Then she began to speak kindly, lovingly, until Rosie was able to sob out some coherence. All Rosie could say was: "He doesn't love me. He just doesn't love me . . . It's impossible for him to love me . . . He won't love me. He won't even talk to me."

As much as she needed to share the total problem, Rosie honored Jerry's secret and refused to tell. What she told was enough, however, to gain the loving response she needed. Marilyn's support enabled her to go on.

The only problem with that one phone conversation was that Jerry overheard it. His anger and fear mounted. He withdrew further into silence until Rosie's frustration was complete. Jerry was the only one she was allowed to talk with about their problem, and now he refused to talk.

Rosie could always tell when Jerry was about to leave the house to "cruise" the streets of Portland. His behavior became predictable; his mood swings widened.

Although she didn't know where he was or who he was with or when he'd be home, she always knew what he was doing.

These nights became "nights of unknowns" to her.

Besides the uncertainties about Jerry's whereabouts, there were concerns of even greater significance to Rosie:

Would he be hurt?

Would he be caught or even arrested?

Would he ask forgiveness?

What would she do if he didn't?

Would she be able to forgive him?

Could she continue to tolerate his behavior?

Could he ever love her or even himself again?

Because she already knew most of the answers to her questions, she would always conclude that she had better prepare herself for the inevitable. She had to be ready when he came home.

Rosie would then pray, "God, I know it's crucial to our marriage that I forgive Jerry. He needs my unconditional love and my unconditional forgiveness. Please enable me tonight to forgive him."

Rosie knew forgiveness. She never once questioned her responsibility to Jerry. She had become a Christian at age twenty and had experienced the unconditional forgiveness of God. She knew what she had to do.

Rosie kept thinking, "Who am I not to forgive Jerry?"

Jerry would move quietly and sullenly back into the house. Rosie's first thought was, "You idiot, when are you going to learn that this really isn't fun? It devastates you. It devastates me. It's destroying us."

But again she forgave him. She not only forgave him, often she would also make love to him. In those early morning hours, the pain, the tears, the disillusionment, the rebellion would be gone. In their place was remorse.

For three-and-a-half years this pattern persisted.

The guilt load again increased.

Rosie's forgiveness persisted.

But Jerry's encounters also persisted.

Rosie became reconciled to the fact that Jerry was gay and that she might be forced to always live with a third person in their marriage. A third person who could never be identified and a person with whom it was impossible to compete.

For Rosie it was three-and-a-half years of torment.

CHAPTER NINE

Three People in Need

Finally they came to see me—together.

They were desperate—but still united. It was not a case of one dragging the other. They shared a sense of urgency. They both felt the need for help.

For Rosie it meant welcome relief. She'd been forced to keep her secret for three-and-a-half years. Now she was able to tell her story.

For Jerry it meant telling his story again. He always resisted that. He had told it so many times and still had not found release. Again he was face to face with the possibility of rejection or even worse, exposure.

I had no idea why they had come. I was still unaware of Jerry's struggle with homosexuality. I saw them regularly at church and viewed them as happy newlyweds. They were active in ministry, serving their growing Sunday school class and working regularly with new Christians.

As they came into my office, I noticed they seemed more subdued than usual.

I began sorting through the possibilities of the reason for this visit.

Was it a problem at work—at home—at church?

Was their marriage solid and intact?

As they were seated side by side, we talked about the wedding, their marriage, the church, their jobs. I kept probing with questions, hoping that I would finally ask the one question that would enable them to address their real reason for coming. The conversation dragged on and on, and all the time the three of us were fully aware that I was unable to determine the problem and that they were unwilling to reveal it.

It was obvious that whatever the problem was, it was serious. The lines of concern were etched on both their faces.

Finally I asked, "Jerry, Rosie, something is troubling you. Would you like to tell me what it is?"

With a nervous laugh, Jerry shifted in his chair, crossed and uncrossed his legs, and then began again playing his verbal games.

After long moments of delay, all the time wringing his hands and Rosie's, he said, "Pastor, I've been struggling with homosexuality all of my life. I thought when Rosie and I were married that that was the end of it.

"I had been celibate for almost a year before our wedding, but by the end of the first three months of marriage, I began to give in to the temptation again."

Rosie was silent—her head bowed, her body tense.

She showed no hint of surprise, just deep concern.

I listened intently, looking from one to the other for confirmation of every word. I watched Rosie's face carefully, convinced that surely she was not aware of all Jerry was telling me. But this wife was no unsuspecting victim.

She knew it all.

She had lived with Jerry through every painful moment. She had stifled the many urges to cry for help. She had been the unwilling but loyal partner in a conspiracy that had fooled everyone. Now the pain of exposure was as great for the wife as it was for her husband.

At times tears filled her eyes. Occasionally she would blush as she listened to her husband recite the details of his encounters with fellow gays.

Every once in a while she would look into Jerry's face with compassion and encouragement. At times she would try to read my responses.

I tried hard not to display any feelings of shock or surprise.

That was difficult. I was both shocked and surprised.

I never once suspected Jerry's problem or the real reason for his withdrawal from seminary. I had taken his explanation at face value. It's not unusual for a seminarian to want relief. Often there are financial needs. At times there is that deep need for diversion, especially when one has been in school as long as Jerry had.

I had always seen Jerry and his parents as deeply committed to Christ, intensely loyal to their church, and spiritual leaders within their families.

He was an outstanding Christian. He was always in the Scriptures. He loved to talk to others about Christ. He was anxious to minister and impatient to return to seminary.

My observations were not imagined. Jerry was not a hypocrite, feigning some false relationship with Jesus Christ. He was genuinely a child of God who loved his Savior. He was real, and as he haltingly labored through his long confession, I was baffled.

I was also stunned that I really didn't know this man whom I thought I knew so well.

"How is it possible for one to love God and be a homosexual?" I thought. "How can one who studies and knows the Bible so well be so disobedient to its teachings?"

As he continued, I found myself becoming increasingly repulsed.

I reflected briefly on the Old Testament story of Sodom and Gomorrah as Jerry rambled on.

Sodom had always seemed to be synonymous with the grossest of evils. Sodom, the city of perversion, with its insatiable lust and its all-consuming cravings was a city completely out of control, a city ripe for judgment. That judgment has always been a frightening reminder of man's limitless potential for sin and God's awesome ability to punish. Homosexuality seemed to be at the core of the entire disaster.

The books of Leviticus, Deuteronomy, Romans, 1 Corinthians, and 1 Timothy warn explicitly against homosexuality.

Though I knew the biblical teaching about homosexuality, I had never been familiar with a homosexual.

Now I was looking at one, listening to one—and realizing that this one was a longtime friend and a dear brother in Christ. I found myself struggling with a set of emotions that were in deep conflict with each other.

As Jerry spoke, I reviewed the events of the past few months, events that brought the world of the gay and the community of the church into sharp conflict in Portland.

Homosexuals seemed to be actively pursuing political acceptance in Portland in much the same way that they had attempted to receive it in San Francisco and in Dade County, Florida.

The homosexual community in Portland was openly claiming one hundred thousand gays in the greater Portland area.

The city had adopted rulings that prohibited discrimination in its hiring practices.

The police department was allegedly recruiting lesbians and gays by welcoming their applications for job openings.[1]

The Buckman neighborhood was being infiltrated by homosexuals. This was especially distasteful to me since Hinson church was located almost dead center in the Buckman area.

The gay community was demanding minority status and pushing the state legislature for laws that would prohibit discrimination.

Oregon's governor had appointed a task force subcommittee on sexual orientation. They were addressed in an open meeting by a spokesman who stated that homosexuality is a normal and natural preference. The panel voted unanimously to recommend legislation that would prevent discrimination against lesbians and male homosexuals. Those bills, in essence, would assure employment and housing to the gay community.

Portland's mayor had declared Gay Pride Day. I hadn't quite made up my mind on gay rights, but I had no struggle whatsoever in opposing gay pride.

I wrote to the mayor, the city council members, and many legislators expressing my concern. Most of the responses I received were unsympathetic to my position.

Limited damage had been done to property owned by the church as our position on what we perceived to be the gay invasion became known.

The very week that Jerry and Rosie came in to see me had been extremely difficult. I had been maligned, misquoted, and had received threatening and obscene phone calls. Political lead-

---

1. *Oregon Gay Rights Report*, June/July, 1977, p. 6.

ers had rebuked me. The Town Council, Portland's gay organization, had written an open letter to the Internal Revenue Service requesting an investigation to determine if Hinson had violated its tax-exempt status by my being so vocal.

I was, to say the least, unsympathetic to the whole homosexual community and found myself becoming increasingly angered by their militant tactics.

And now right in front of me sat one of my dearest friends, one of Hinson's active workers, acknowledging that he had been a practicing homosexual for more than twenty years.

I became more and more uneasy as Jerry spoke. I fidgeted. I inwardly fumed. I restrained myself as long as possible. Finally I looked up and stared long and hard into the face of this hurting man. "Jerry, stop right there—that's enough—I've had it up to my eyeballs this week with gays!"

The words shot out from my lips like miniature cannonballs, blasting with explosive force on the unsuspecting ears of two people who had never expected such a response.

All of my restrained emotions had erupted in just one moment. They scattered debris all over this couple who had come to me with such high hope.

The room fell silent.

Both Jerry and Rosie looked at me with dismay and then lowered their eyes. Was it possible that their own pastor couldn't understand? Was it possible that the one person from whom they least expected rejection had rejected them?

Blushing, I searched for something to say.

I sensed fear.

I sensed disappointment.

I sensed withdrawal.

I remained seated behind my desk for a long time.

Finally I said, "Jerry, Rosie, I'm sorry. Please forgive me. I really don't think my words were directed at you nearly as much as they were at the frustrating events of this past week."

I then explained what had been happening. "I guess I really don't understand. I have seen homosexuality only as a blight that needs to be removed—an evil that needs to be extinguished. I've never before seen it as a problem that needs to be addressed or a power that needs to be conquered. I've not seen it as a habit from which individuals crave deliverance or as a sin for which one pleads forgiveness."

I asked Jerry to tell me more. As he did, I was overwhelmed with my own lack of love and concern for a segment of society that needed help. A group of thousands who wanted help. People whose cries had made strange sounds and whose pleas had taken on peculiar forms as they suggested that they liked their life style and even recommended it to others. People caught in a trap.

I felt helpless, totally helpless, to offer any hope to any one of them.

I came out from behind my desk, took Jerry's and Rosie's hands in mine, knelt down beside their chairs, and asked God for forgiveness and for grace for the three of us, each caught in a trap. Grace that we might be freed to demonstrate the power of the loving Christ to those who were powerless.

We wept together as we shared the helplessness we felt.

It was no longer just a homosexual who craved freedom from his habit or a wife who sought deliverance for her husband. It was also a pastor who sought freedom from a fear and from a revulsion that had invaded his soul and had made a redemptive ministry to this imprisoned group an impossibility.

CHAPTER TEN

Just Another Sin?

I needed to learn more about homosexuality and I needed to learn it fast. Jerry was coming back, and he deserved more from me than just an emotional response to his problem.

The homosexual community has a name for people like me—*homophobic* or one who fears homosexuality. For some reason my emotional responses to homosexuality were different from my responses to other sins. My feelings were not unlike those of many in the Christian community.

Whether we fear the militant nature of this subculture or their evangelistic zeal in making converts or the threat of losing our children to them, I really don't know. Many of us are downright scared by the spread of diseases that seem to be related to the practice. Some fear that God's judgment may fall on a nation that tolerates such behavior. Others of us may have an indefinable fear that we ourselves are possibly latent homosexuals.

Whatever the reason, many of us are afraid, and our fears make it difficult to minister. The church is called a redemptive society and is usually noted for its aggressive action against sin, but the homosexual battlefield is one that we have neglected. We have permitted Satan to take his prisoners and have assumed them to be lost forever.

We have treated homosexuals as lepers. We consider them

unclean and fear that even their touch will render us tainted for life.

Some of these thoughts were brought into focus during a meeting between Portland's mayor and a number of concerned local pastors. After he was deluged with negative responses to his declaration of a gay pride day, the mayor had arranged the meeting.

He explained his position.

We explained ours.

Finally he asked, "If homosexuality is the threat to Portland you say it is, what are you doing about it?"

None of us had an answer. We had developed no strategy; we were providing no solution.

Why? I'm not sure—unless we were still viewing it as an enemy to be feared rather than a need to be addressed.

My church was reacting to the issue as far as the ballot box was concerned, but there had been no concerted effort to confront and grapple with the root problem and its far-reaching implications.

If I was going to do something, I needed to know more. Liberal and gay theologians were trying to pull the teeth out of many biblical statements. I was being intimidated by statistics that suggested a vast and veritable army was about to attack.

I was watching some of my people slip away into the enemy's camp.

And then there was Jerry . . .

He needed help.

He wanted help.

He was pleading for help, and I had no choice but to give it to him.

I read.

I studied.

I accumulated a small library of books, books by psychiatrists, psychologists, doctors, teachers, gays, and ex-gays. Some were secular and some were Christian.

My reading provided many answers but also opened up more questions. There was little agreement from society in general. There was even confusion within the Christian community.

I needed more than answers; I needed *right* answers.

As always, I was driven back to the Scriptures.

Ten books of the Bible give us information regarding homosexuality.

Genesis records the sin and subsequent judgment of the cities of Sodom and Gomorrah (Genesis 18:20-19:25).

Leviticus defines homosexuality as a sin that is characteristic of pagan cultures. It is prohibited in Israel by Mosaic law (Leviticus 18:22, 24).

Deuteronomy forbids the practice of sodomy and also forbids the use of wages earned in the practice to be given as an offering to the Lord (Deuteronomy 23:17, 18).

Judges reveals homosexuality within the Israelite culture (Judges 19:22-27).

First Kings exposes one of Israel's kings as encouraging the pagan practice of homosexuality (1 Kings 14:21-24).

Romans traces the practice of homosexuality in humanity and defines the practice as the final step in humanity's decline (Romans 1:18-27).

First Corinthians names homosexuality as one characteristic of the unsaved who are forbidden entrance into the kingdom of God (1 Corinthians 6:9-11).

First Timothy describes homosexuality as being characteristic of the lawless and the ungodly (1 Timothy 1:10).

Second Peter refers to Sodom and Gomorrah as an example of God's righteous judgment upon sin (2 Peter 2:6-9).

Jude uses Sodom and Gomorrah as an example of God's judgment upon all sin (Jude 7).

The above passages locate homosexuality in both Old and New Testament cultures. God's judgment is imposed wherever the sin is found.

Those passages confirm that homosexuality is pagan, unnatural, sinful, contrary to the moral nature of God, and deserving of divine judgment.

Romans 1:18-32 speaks to the question of cause. Is homosexuality genetic or behavioral? Is it inherent or is it learned? Is it hormonal or is it habitual?

The passage teaches that:

humanity instinctively, intuitively, knew God (1:19, 20);
humanity willfully rejected God (1:21);
humanity exchanged a Spirit-God for a god of flesh (1:23);

> flesh then became god and the lusts of the flesh became supreme (1:24-32).

Humanity's long-range experience is similar to the individual pattern. Homosexuality is a learned behavior that degenerates through repeated practice until it becomes rooted in nature and character.

First Corinthians 6:9-11 not only locates homosexuality in the Greek culture but also describes some members of the local church as being former homosexuals.

"Or do you not know that the unrighteous shall not inherit the kingdom of God? Do not be deceived;

neither fornicators,
nor idolators,
nor adulterers,
nor effeminate,
nor homosexuals,
nor thieves,
nor the covetous,
nor drunkards,
nor revilers,
nor swindlers,

shall inherit the kingdom of God. And such were some of you; but you were washed, but you were sanctified, but you were justified in the name of the Lord Jesus Christ, and in the Spirit of our God."

I am familiar with the passage. I have preached it many times. As I studied it, however, I found that it suggests things about homosexuality that I hadn't really noticed before.

It suggests that homosexuality is no worse than other sins. Homosexuality is buried in the catalogue of sins. It is placed alongside thievery and drunkenness, suggesting that it is neither the greatest nor the least of all offensive practices in humanity.

It provides hope for the homosexual. Homosexuals can change—or rather can be changed. The phrase "such were some of you" places all these sinful life styles in the past tense. The popular notion that homosexuals are locked permanently into a life style that cannot be changed is simply one more lie of Satan.

It portrays the church as being populated by ex-gays. Each of the ten sinful practices characterized the former life style of some

member of the early church. This means that not only can homosexuals be changed, they can also be forgiven.

It even records some of the steps out of homosexuality. The words "you were washed" suggest cleansing. Cleansing always requires the active participation of the one being washed. A homosexual, like any other sinner, must admit to his need for cleansing and then submit to the process, no matter how long or how painful it may be.

The words "you were sanctified" speak to a homosexual's need for acceptance—one of the most powerful and universal needs among the homosexual community. To be sanctified means to be set apart for God, or to be God's property. God accepts completely and totally whatever is given to him. In sanctification God says, "You are mine."

The words "you were justified" deal with the crippling problem of self-image. A homosexual, like any other sinner who has accepted divine forgiveness, stands before God as one who has never sinned. He is no longer obsessed with his failure; he is aware that his former life is gone.

He is now a new person with new potentials and new desires. In justification God says, "You are all right."

It reveals the sources of help that are available. "In the name of the Lord Jesus Christ" draws our attention to the authority figure who is capable of rebuking and limiting the satanic or demonic forces that may be at work in the homosexual's body.

"In the Spirit of our God" places the focus on the indwelling companion who is able to provide such internal resources as spiritual energy, contentment, satisfaction, and peace. The Spirit of God is the one who changes attitudes and desires. He is the one who makes homosexuality repulsive and holiness attractive.

The act of homosexuality, its ensuing guilt, and its compelling habitual life style are all dealt with in the redemptive work of Jesus Christ.

The emotional complications that a homosexual experiences may not disappear immediately, but the power to change is inherent in Jesus Christ.

In a later discussion Jerry asked me, "Pastor, why didn't you use 1 Corinthians 6:9-11 in our discussions together? I needed the hope it offered, but you never mentioned it."

I didn't have an answer. I really didn't know unless possibly

the message of judgment in the passage had always been more important to me than the message of hope.

"Sodom and Gomorrah" often suggests that homosexuality is the grossest of evils simply because of the enormity and swiftness of God's judgment. Other cultures and whole civilizations, however, have experienced similar judgments.

I have seen the probable location of ancient Sodom, but I have also seen the ruins of Capernaum. Peter's hometown on the northern tip of the Sea of Galilee is never mentioned as a breeding place for immorality, and yet its judgment, according to Jesus, would be even worse than that of Sodom and Gomorrah.[1] Why? Not because of homosexuality but because of unbelief.

Chorazin and Bethsaida were judged because they refused to repent of their unbelief.[2]

Jerusalem was destroyed, not because of its immorality—it had strongly enforced laws against homosexuality—but because of its rejection of Christ.[3]

Homosexuality is not the worst sin. It is possibly no worse than any other sin. But it *is* sin, and God hates all sin and ultimately judges all sin.

Like any other sin, however, it is forgiveable.

And homosexuals are people. I had forgotten that. They are people with a problem.

People who are made in the image of God.

People who have eternal souls.

People who have fallen into the snare of sin.

People who are worthy of our time and attention.

People whom God loves.

People for whom Jesus died.

People who will populate heaven because of the love and forgiveness of God.

Some time later in an open meeting with Portland's militant gay community, I saw them—really saw them—for the first time.

I saw them as boys and girls and sons and daughters.

I saw them as Christians and non-Christians.

I looked into their eyes and saw beyond their hate. I saw their anguish, their frustration, their despair, their fear.

---

1. Matthew 11:24
2. Matthew 11:21
3. Matthew 23:37-24:2

I saw the perpetual pleading that speaks so much louder than their angry words.

I have long since forgotten their arguments, but cannot forget their fears or their faces. The faces of people who need help. The faces of prisoners staring blankly from between the bars of moral enslavement. The faces of the helpless who are sobbing way down deep inside of themselves for someone to truly love them, to understand them, and to care for them.

Jerry opened my eyes to see not homosexuals, but *people*. People who are trapped by homosexuality and want their freedom.

As I continued to study and reflect, I noticed something else of great importance to me—the people who were really helping Jerry seemed to know the least about homosexuality.

But they did know a lot about compassion—and commitment—and love—and prayer—and Jesus.

They were tenacious and determined and available.

They were accepting and involved. Convinced that freedom was available, they hung on until it was experienced—and sometimes that took a long, long time.

As homosexuality and sin and people and grace and forgiveness and God's power came into clear focus, Jerry's problem fell into place as just another sin—a sin that deserved my attention and needed God's help.

CHAPTER ELEVEN

A Change in Thinking

I'm a very poor long-term counselor. Three sessions are about all I can handle. If a counselee does not show any marked progress by that time, I usually refer him to someone else.

I told this to Jerry as we set up a schedule of counseling sessions. His initial response was disappointment. He felt let down. He believed that I had made a long-term commitment to him and he had begun looking forward to a relationship that I found impossible to provide.

I recommended Joel. Jerry was quick to tell me that he didn't like the prospect of telling his story again. But he agreed to the suggestion, and after spending a few sessions together, strengthening our biblical orientation on the subjects of sin, forgiveness, and deliverance, Jerry finally made his first appointment to see Joel MacDonald.

Joel was a member of the staff at Hinson, a husband, a father, and a former naval officer. He knew Jerry and Rosie well. He had attended seminary with Jerry and had been the leader of a growth group to which the couple belonged.

Jerry's story came as a complete surprise to him also. He responded to it much better than I, though.

Jerry was immediately impressed by Joel's genuine empathy and compassion.

Joel committed himself to Jerry and began to lay down a simple plan designed to help his friend. Joel was not any more knowledgeable about homosexuality than I had been, but as the minister of discipleship, he knew the importance of moving alongside another's life. He knew the necessity of the twin strategies of availability and accountability.

They agreed to a long-term, once-a-week counseling relationship—at no charge. Included in their sessions was accountability (each time they met, Joel would ask pointedly, "Have you engaged in homosexuality this week?") and Scripture memorization.

Jerry finally relaxed with the feeling that someone who was always accessible had a genuine interest in him. That genuine interest coupled with Joel's willingness to freely give to Jerry the large hunks of time he demanded became a strong deterrent to Jerry's homosexual encounters.

Jerry did not like to have to admit defeat. He also found it extremely difficult to lie to Joel. He did lie occasionally, but it was not long before he found this impossible.

Joel was more than a counselor. He became a close friend and companion. He was not just seeking information or an academic adventure. When Joel said, "Feel free to call on me," he meant it. He kept his schedule somewhat flexible and made himself more available than any of Jerry's previous counselors.

He was interested in everything that interested Jerry. There were times they didn't even discuss Jerry's problem. They talked about his work, his marriage, his family, and they always spent time reviewing the passages memorized during that week.

Jerry finally had someone with whom he could freely share all of his feelings, his thoughts, his actions. He would describe his guilt, his shame, and his despair.

The relationship became so nonthreatening that Jerry felt the freedom to simply tell his counselor to quit preaching and listen. Many times Jerry would say, "Will you please be quiet and let me say what I'm feeling. I've just got to get this out!"

There were times when Jerry would sit across from Joel in stark, cold silence—unwilling and unable to speak. He would be resistant to Joel's quiet manner and withdraw into the seclusion of his own troubled mind.

Joel would simply say, "That's okay, Jerry—you don't have

to talk if you don't want to. I'll talk. You're free to leave anytime you wish."

The sessions would always end on a positive note of hope as Joel would conclude by saying, "Jerry, you realize what the Scriptures say, don't you?" He would then reach for his Bible, flip open the pages to an appropriate passage, and read.

Then they would pray—for forgiveness and for strength.

Joel is the only one who took the time to talk to Rosie privately. "Rosie, you're an incredible wife for not leaving Jerry. So many would have hit the road long before now."

This reinforcement was just what Rosie needed, and it gave her fresh courage to continue.

Joel and Dan Britts were the two most memorable companions who walked with Jerry. Neither of them knew much if anything about homosexuality. Both, however, knew the meaning of commitment.

It was a concern to me that both Jerry and Rosie were actively involved in discipling new Christians. They would meet a new believer and stay with him through the act of believer's baptism.

Because of the public aspect of that ministry, I asked Jerry one day how he was doing in his struggle. He lowered his eyes and acknowledged that he was not always successful in overcoming the powerful temptation that haunted him.

"What if a young believer should be just finding his way out of the homosexual community and should recognize you as gay?" I asked.

He was silent.

"Jerry," I said, "I'm so proud of the progress you're making, but I think that it would be best if you gave up your place of ministry until you have this thing completely under control. In fact, I see no option at the present time."

Rosie thought my action was harsh but appropriate. Working with new Christians was the one ministry that gave her great joy.

She became angry with Jerry as she began to feel the limitation that his sin placed upon them both.

Jerry, however, felt that I was justified in my discipline. He told me later that he was actually relieved that I had the courage to take that kind of action.

The decision to remove them from this place of service was sobering. The action didn't stop Jerry from his encounters, but both Jerry and Rosie point to this experience of limited discipline as a significant point in Jerry's life.

Oftentimes Jerry would say to Rosie:

"My pastor has disciplined me."

"I'm no longer allowed to serve."

"I've been asked to resign from the discipleship committee."

"I can't even hold an office in my church."

Jerry was finally beginning to see the ugliness of sin.

His encounters became fewer.

It was during this time that Jerry and Rosie's Sunday school teacher challenged the Sunday school class to memorize the New Testament book of Philippians. Jerry and Rosie took up the challenge and spent their commuting time memorizing Scripture. It came hard at first.

Four chapters, one hundred and four verses—a significant project—and a life-changing one.

Philippians has much to say about right thinking. Jerry soon realized that his thought life was a black and white issue. Impure thinking is displeasing to God. Pure thoughts are not only delightful to God, they are also catalysts for right actions.

Sin begins in the mind, and Jerry needed a transformed mind if he was going to experience a changed life.

It took a long time, coupled with constant review, to memorize Philippians. With amazement Jerry one day exclaimed, "Rosie, memorizing Scripture is changing my thinking!"

CHAPTER TWELVE

"Can the Church Handle This?"

For three years Rosie continued to help Jerry in his relentless struggle to break free from homosexuality.

Jerry counseled regularly with Joel.

Rosie persisted in her support of her husband.

They both memorized Scripture daily.

At midpoint in this three-year time span, Jerry's homosexual encounters ceased. He dared not claim deliverance—he had done that before. He did enjoy some restrained hope that maybe—just maybe—he could someday claim to be an ex-gay.

There are those who have claimed immediate and complete deliverance from homosexuality, but most, like Jerry, have learned that genuine deliverance is a slow, agonizingly painful process with the ever-present fear of falling at any time.

At the end of eighteen months of freedom, Jerry and Rosie again called me for an appointment.

I met them at the door, hugged them both, asked what I could do for them, and laughingly cautioned Jerry to keep it brief—which he did.

"Pastor, I'd like to ask a favor," said Jerry. "Rosie and I have been talking about the possibility of sharing my testimony publicly here at Hinson. This is not just a spur-of-the-moment idea—it's actually something that we have prayed and thought about for

a long time. We are not in total agreement about it. We need your advice as to whether or not this is appropriate or if the timing is right."

We sat down. I studied both faces for just a moment and was amazed at the distinct contrast from what I remembered three years before. They were relaxed—Jerry was not fidgeting—and they appeared happy and at peace.

"Why do you want to do this?" I asked.

Jerry thought for a few moments and then said, "I can think of four reasons. I want to seek the church's forgiveness. Very few people know that I've been living a double life. I have sinned against God and against Rosie, but I have also sinned against the church. I would like to acknowledge my rebellion openly and feel their forgiveness.

"I would like to know if Hinson church could still accept me if they were to know the ugliest part of my life.

"I also have a strong desire to praise God for what he has done for me.

"I think the strongest reason for asking this is that I want to offer encouragement and hope to any homosexual who is struggling as I have been. I am living proof that it is possible for a homosexual to change—I want the Christian community to know that, I want the non-Christian community to know that, I want the gay community to know that."

I couldn't resist Jerry's enthusiasm—but I did have to question it.

"Jerry," I said, "this could be a test to determine if this church is really a redemptive body. I wish I could assure you of the outcome. It's possible that this church cannot handle this. They may find it impossible to forgive you. You have been leading a double life before them for years. They may be angered by this. Are you willing for that sort of rejection?"

"We are willing to take that risk," he said.

"It may be that the reaction would be just the opposite. This church may forgive you, wrap their arms around you, and accept you completely," I added. "I really don't know what will happen."

There was good reason for my uncertainty. The struggle between the gay and nongay had reached a peak.

I had circulated a letter signed by a number of Christian lead-

ers that listed the names of political aspirants who were endorsed by the gay community. Both the gay community and the politicians were angry. We were engaged in a running battle that would continue right up to election day. With feelings running so high, I wasn't sure that the timing was right.

I asked Rosie, "How do you feel about this?"

"I'm not sure, Pastor," she answered. "Let's not make a decision right now. Why don't we go home and pray about it? We'll let you know by Saturday morning."

As we walked down the stairs, I sensed that Rosie was more than just hesitant—she was frightened.

The next morning Rosie was fixing breakfast when Jerry came into the kitchen. Her first words were, "Why don't you call Pastor and tell him that you'll be sharing tomorrow morning?"

Jerry was startled. Since leaving my office they had not even discussed the subject.

Rosie explained that she had awakened with a sense of peace. She knew that Jerry needed to do this if he was ever going to heal. "And besides, Jerry, I know you're just busting to get this out."

Jerry and I met on Saturday in preparation for Sunday. We discussed some key questions about homosexuality. He then went home only to stay awake for the rest of the night.

On Sunday morning Jerry was completely consumed with the moment at hand.

He was nervous.

He was excited.

But he was at peace.

CHAPTER THIRTEEN

Exposure

It was Mother's Day. I was continuing a series of sermons on prayer. The emphasis that Sunday was that nothing—absolutely nothing—was beyond the reach of prayer.

I had chosen a number of real-life illustrations to describe the power of prayer, but I needed one more—a clincher. Something to move prayer into everyday living and display its power in a way that was beyond question.

I wanted also to relate my message to mothers.

Jerry was the link I needed. A living example of prayer's delivering power and the son of a mother who had faithfully held him up before the Lord for thirty-five years.

She was there to my left in the second row. She sat in the same seat during each of the three services that morning.

She didn't know that her son was about to reveal the most haunting secret of his lifetime.

Jerry had asked me if he should tell her. I had said, "No." I'm not sure why, and I'm also uncertain as to the wisdom of that decision.

She sat next to her son, and during the opening moments of the first service she displayed the joy and the pride a mother always feels on such an occasion. She did not suspect what was about to happen.

Jerry's father was in Alaska.

In spite of his uncontrollable excitement, Jerry was at peace—so was Rosie.

I probably felt more anxiety than anyone.

Was I doing the right thing for Jerry?

Was it the right thing for my church?

Would Jerry be accepted or rejected—or worse—just tolerated?

Would these people be able to forgive?

Would they be critical for not removing him from the church years earlier?

Would his mother survive this day?

Was Jerry's ministry finished—or just beginning?

I preached for nearly twenty minutes. I repeatedly emphasized prayer's life-changing power.

In the balcony were two members of the gay activist community monitoring my every word. Little did they realize what they were about to hear.

At the appropriate moment I said, "I have one more illustration—a story from real life—a story with real flesh and blood and dressed in real clothing—a story that speaks for itself."

I asked Jerry to come to the platform. I followed him with my eyes as he stood to his feet, slipped out from behind the pew, and began his long walk to the pulpit.

His mother glowed.

His wife prayed.

His friends wondered.

I feared what was about to happen.

As he approached the pulpit, I put my arms around him and said, "I love you, Jerry, and I'm praying for you."

My introduction was brief. "Most of you know Jerry. He has been a member since he came to Portland to attend Western Seminary nine years ago. He attended seminary until March, 1974, and then left school for reasons he will explain in just a few moments.

"Jerry has something to tell you. It will surprise you. It will shock you. It will also encourage greater faith in the power of life-changing prayer."

Jerry grabbed both sides of the pulpit firmly, looked at me, then at his wife and at his mother, heaved a great sigh and began. His face was flushed. Beads of perspiration stood out on his forehead as he spoke.

"Where do I begin? I'll start off by saying, 'Good-morning.' I asked Pastor Baker if I could share my testimony with you this morning, and I'm grateful to him for saying 'Yes.'

"I have wanted to tell you this before, but the timing was not right. God has made it clear that now is the time."

He stopped and sighed again. "What I will be sharing with you this morning is the biggest problem—the biggest battle in my life."

There was another long pause followed by another heavy sigh.

The audience was silent—waiting—wondering.

Jerry then said, "The biggest battle in my life is this—I have been a homosexual almost all my life . . . "

There it was. In just nine words and in just as many seconds as it took to say them, Jerry had done the very thing he had feared most for a lifetime: he exposed the great sin that he had fought so hard to hide.

In just nine words he had told his mother, his friends, one thousand worshipers, and possibly fifty thousand radio listeners that he was a homosexual.

The quiet crowd became even quieter. No one stirred, no one coughed, no one spoke. I watched for reactions. Some faces displayed visible amazement. Others revealed concern. Some heads bowed. Some eyes closed. Some shoulders sagged. Some feet scraped nervously. Some eyes became moist, but no one dabbed at the tears.

I looked in the direction of the mother of the day. She turned white but continued to look at her son as he stood unmasked and vulnerable before the waiting crowd.

Rosie continued to pray.

Jerry addressed the obvious as he said, "As I look around at people's faces, some look puzzled, some confused, other are expressing hostility, amazement. The whole gamut of emotions is displayed when the word *homosexual* is spoken.

"My first experience with homosexuality occurred when I was about nine years old. I didn't know it was a sin. All I knew was that my conscience told me it was something I shouldn't be doing.

"I was a Christian. I had received Jesus Christ into my life when I was six years old. I have never doubted the reality of my relationship with Jesus Christ.

"My homosexuality was not from God. I was not born a homosexual. I believe the Scriptures are very clear in saying that God is perfect, he is holy, and he is just. God created man in his own image. It would be a contradiction for a holy God to create a homosexual.

"I chose it—gradually, progressively, and repeatedly.

"This progressed from grade school through junior high and high school until it became an obsession with me. It became worse during my time in the army.

"Upon completion of my military service I entered seminary.

"I was so excited about being in an atmosphere surrounded by love and a knowledge of the Word. I was sure my battle was over. It wasn't.

"Those three years in seminary were three of the best and yet three of the worst of my life.

"One would think that in seminary of all places I should have felt the freedom to speak up and say, 'Hey, I'm hurting—I need help—I'm fighting for my very existence—surely there is somebody here who can come up with the solution to my problem. If it can't be found here, I can't see any reason to continue living.' I sat in chapel; I sat in the classroom, just as I have sat in this church Sunday after Sunday and cried out quietly, 'O God, where are you?'

"I'd listen to the sermons—to the lectures—" and Jerry stopped. The tears began to flow. He found it difficult to speak. "Not every day was like a funeral. There were days when God would fill me with his joy. Some days the Scriptures would be especially precious, but every day in chapel I'd listen and then I'd want to jump up and shout: 'Hey, who are we kidding?' Why can't we take off some of these masks we are wearing? Why can't we say where we're really hurting?' "

Jerry paused and heaved another sigh in an attempt to bring himself back under control.

"I was desperate—I wanted to tell you how much I needed your help, but I couldn't.

"But I guess it just wasn't proper to mention homosexuality in public. Homosexuality is one of the most feared, most misunderstood subjects in our society.

"It's almost comparable to leprosy. We're treated as nonentities, nonpeople, animals.

"More than anything else in my life, I have fought to keep this a secret.

"I was convinced that the only way I could be accepted was to remain hidden. I was sure that no one would love me if they knew.

"In the years of seminary, with access to all of the knowledge and love that was available, my encounters increased.

"I was desperate. I couldn't continue. I withdrew from school and almost killed myself.

"There were many things that sustained me during that critical time—the knowledge that God loved me and that I was his child in spite of my sin, the people who knew and were counseling me, the power of prayer."

Here he told the powerful story of Dan Britts's confrontation and how it began to change his life.

"And," he added, "I have learned to cry out on my own: 'Help me, Lord.'

"For nearly two years now I've been enjoying victory over the practice of homosexuality. To me that's a miracle. I attribute that totally to God.

"The God of the impossible has done the impossible in my life.

"The one great concern I have is for your forgiveness. I have sinned against God. He has forgiven me. I have sinned against my wife. She has forgiven me. I have sinned against my church family. I would like your forgiveness.

"I'm sorry—please forgive me."

Jerry bowed his head. His body shook. His hands were white as he gripped the sides of the pulpit.

I walked up beside him, put my arm around him, and said, "You have heard Jerry's story, you have listened as his heart and soul have spoken to you. He has requested something from you in return.

"Can you forgive him? Will you forgive him?"

There was a long and frightening silence. Then a voice—"Amen," it said rather quietly. Then another, louder, and another and another and then the audience began to applaud—not for sin, but for a sinner who had dared to ask forgiveness and give God glory for a changed life. A sinner who dared to believe that his friends were strong enough to forgive him, to accept him in

spite of his past, and to love him in spite of his weakness.

Jerry had told it all—and all that he told was heard and all that was heard was forgiven.

CHAPTER FOURTEEN

"I'm Proud to Have a Son Like You."

I looked again into the face of Jerry's mother. Her head was still erect. Her body hadn't moved. Her expression was the same. Her color was back. She shifted slightly to let her son regain his seat and then responded quickly to his touch as Jerry put his arms around the women who had prayed for him so long.

Rosie's head was high. Her smile was radiant. Her victory was complete.

I turned my back to the audience and wept—three times that morning.

There really wasn't much more to do.

We stood—we sang—we prayed—we left.

The same thing happened in each service.

The first man to reach Jerry at the close of the early service was a well-dressed businessman—not a close friend—just a casual acquaintance.

"Jerry," he said. "I do forgive you. I love you. We all have areas of sin that we could confess, but we don't all have the courage to do it."

At the close of the second service, a friend with whom Jerry had been having some conflict rushed up in tears, hugged him close, and fighting for words said, "Of course I forgive you, Jerry, and I'm available to help you any time you need me . . . and I would really like to be your friend."

A young couple, newly married, caught Jerry at the close of the final service. The wife was visibly shaken and in tears; she was unable to speak. She hugged him and finally said, "I can't believe you've been going through all of this alone. We were such close friends and we were totally unaware of your struggle."

A retired school principal and long-time friend took Jerry's hand firmly in his own and with tears in his eyes said, "I have just heard a great man."

The beginning of both the second and third service was delayed due to the crowd that flocked to reassure Jerry and Rosie.

His mother hugged him and said, "I love you, Jerry."

After listening to a tape recording of the service, his father called and said, "Jerry, I'm very proud to have a son like you—I love you very much and only wish I could have been there with your mother."

Jerry had been anxiously waiting for his father's response. When it came, he was greatly relieved. It was one of the first times he had ever felt genuine unconditional acceptance from the one man he had truly loved all his life.

The overall response was positive and enthusiastic . . . but it was not unanimous.

Shaking his head from side to side, one man walked by me and said, "Pastor, how could you have done such a thing? That was wrong—terribly wrong."

Another refused to shake my hand as I offered it.

A woman said, "I'm so ashamed to have been here this morning."

Most of the letters were positive. Those who objected did so vigorously.

One letter stated, "I suppose we're going to start turning Hinson into a gay church now. I can't believe that you encouraged those words this morning. I'm not sure that I want to continue bringing my children to Hinson."

Most of Jerry and Rosie's friends remained close. Some withdrew. Some of those from whom Jerry had expected the greatest support became very clumsy in their relationship. Most of us, however, felt great joy and relief that a sinner's battles were being won for a change.

Jerry had no sooner concluded his testimony of deliverance than the church phones began ringing.

People throughout the state had heard the broadcast. Many of them responded. Some called to encourage Jerry, others to thank him for his message of hope. Some asked for help.

One of the first to call had been listening on a portable radio while sailing up the Columbia River. He could not believe that this sort of message was coming from Hinson.

He called on his ship-to-shore phone to confirm the origin of the broadcast and then left his phone number for Jerry.

He was gay, tired of his life style, and wanted help.

Following the morning service, Jerry called him and set up an appointment to see him the next evening.

Jerry visited the caller with a friend and led him to Jesus Christ.

CHAPTER FIFTEEN

A New Life, a New Ministry

Other homosexuals began calling Jerry—not for an encounter but for help.

Many expressed that his message of hope was the first they had ever heard. His offer of help was the first they had ever received.

They asked for advice, for encouragement, and for time.

Wives of homosexuals asked how they could help their husbands.

Lesbians called to ask for help.

Their conversations were always guarded—their requests always masked, just as Jerry's had been. They too feared rejection and exposure.

Jerry and Rosie responded immediately—enthusiastically.

Soon they were deluged. It became impossible to answer every need individually.

"Reconciliation" was the answer.

That was the name they gave to their group—a small gathering of men and women who began moving out of their places of hiding into a fellowship of struggling people who were finally ready to admit their need for help.

They met each week.

Their average attendance was not large, but their numbers grew. Their potential was awesome.

A camaraderie developed. A close kinship followed. Their dependence upon one another became so great that continued and consistant meetings were essential.

Jerry and Rosie's time was stretched—their energies depleted—their knowledge was taxed.

Hinson church sent them to attend a seminar in San Rafael, California. It was hosted by a group called Love in Action. It had been organized in 1973 as an outreach to those who had found their homosexuality to be incompatible with their Christian beliefs.

They learned proven techniques for counseling. They heard other exciting success stories. They found that God's great delivering power was not limited to one lone couple in the Pacific Northwest. People all over the country were having similar experiences. Many were finding freedom.

With a better understanding of the causes and cures for homosexuality, they returned and poured themselves into the lives of others.

Though they were both working at full-time jobs, they gave every spare moment—their days off, their evenings, and often their nights to the hurting.

They met with the staff of the church and a number of deacons. With them were a number of the members of Reconciliation who had been receiving their help.

For some it was the first time that they had sat together with known homosexuals. One man turned to me and whispered, "They look just like people."

We listened as Jerry told what was happening. We were pleased as counselors commended Jerry for his work. We were enthralled as homosexuals and their wives openly shared how God was using Jerry in their lives.

Some had been spared from suicide. Families were being restored. Wives were gaining understanding and hope. Some homosexuals were experiencing freedom.

One of the group who sat across the room from me began to speak. I had seen him in church. He was handsome, married, a father—and a homosexual.

His first words to us were, "Man, this is the biggest group of straight people I've ever told about my homosexuality."

We all laughed—nervously at first and then with great relief.

He told us his story.

He had considered suicide many times.

He had paid out eighty dollars a visit for psychiatric help that didn't help.

His mental health was "like a yo-yo."

His self-image was "that of a snake."

He had considered becoming a Christian, but believed that he needed to "clean up his act" first.

Then he met Jerry and Rosie. They accepted him immediately.

Jerry gave him a Bible and invited him to church. Jerry sat with him, sang with him, prayed with him, and even held his hand during conversational prayer.

He trusted Jesus Christ and began to grow.

Later I baptized him.

Even later he was elected as the president of his Sunday school class and started influencing others toward a life of freedom.

Martha and I visited Reconciliation.

As the group gathered I felt uneasy. This was a new experience and admittedly threatening.

There were people in attendance who knew all about my past militant anti-homosexual position. There were also those who had been militant gays.

We sat together in Jerry and Rosie's family room. A room that had formerly been a double garage but was remodeled to meet the needs of an expanding ministry.

We sang to the accompaniment of a guitar.

Each one introduced himself to us.

Jerry asked if anyone was hurting.

They began sharing problems with work, with family, with friends. Some needed prayer to help find employment.

Each problem was individually prayed for.

Jerry then explained why we were there. We wanted to learn more about them—we wanted to help them—we wanted to understand them.

I told them that I was writing a book about Jerry and Rosie and the church and God and gays and hope.

I asked permission to read the first three chapters to them—the chapters that described Jerry's struggles, his withdrawal from

seminary, and his eventual desire to die.

As I read the room became deathly silent. Some turned pale, others began to weep. I was just beginning to read the third chapter when one young man interrupted and said, "Sir, may I ask a favor of you? Will you please not read any more?"

I stopped, surprised.

I asked, "Why don't you want me to read this to you?"

"It hurts too much. It's too painful. In describing Jerry's struggle you're forcing us to relive our own struggles, and I just can't handle that tonight."

Others were quick to agree. They all wanted me to stop.

I closed my notebook, laid it on the floor, and felt the relief that comes with understanding. Jerry's story was not just his story, it was their story. It portrayed the real life encounter of a number of struggling homosexuals. They had identified with it almost immediately.

For the rest of the evening Martha and I were no longer strangers. We felt no rejection. We were accepted.

The members of the group freely shared their stories, their fears, their hopes, their loves, their hates.

They expressed their dismay at having a preacher in their midst—even one who was willing to listen rather than just anxious to speak.

I admitted my ignorance.

I acknowledged my fears.

I openly stated my feelings of rejection.

I asked their forgiveness.

They told us how they all felt rejected by the church.

They resented the lack of compassion they sensed from the Christian community.

They felt bitterness toward what they described as a double standard for Christians. A double standard that was tolerant of some sins and intolerant of others.

They were all anxious to change.

None of them denied that homosexuality was sin.

All of them wanted to feel acceptance and to enjoy deliverance.

Only eight of them attended church.

To continue to practice homosexuality they either had to block-out truth, change their theology, or pretend they had no

problem. They could not acknowledge their sin publicly without experiencing the rejection of the Christian community.

Many of them had been rejected completely by their families.

Some had been unable to tell their parents.

One woman stated that to tell her mother that she was a lesbian would probably have caused her mother to kill herself.

Others had told their parents. Some parents found it impossible to accept the fact of their child's homosexuality.

One man whose father was a pastor had finally summoned enough courage to tell his dad. They were in the garage working together on the family car.

"Dad," he said.

"What is it son?" the father answered without looking up from his work.

"I've got something to tell you—it's very important," he said—haltingly.

"Go ahead, son, I'm listening."

"Dad—I'm a homosexual," the boy finally said.

The father continued his work on the engine without any response.

The son waited—and waited—and waited.

The father said nothing until he straightened up, looked in his son's direction and said, "Hand me that screwdriver, will you?"

The father took the tool from his son's hand, leaned down under the hood, and continued to work, completely ignoring his son's frightening admission.

The boy never mentioned his problem again. His father never acknowledged that he had heard him.

Many expressed their desire for a Christian man to display a father image to them.

Many wanted someone to confront them and to hold them accountable.

Others just wanted to know that someone somewhere was praying for them.

One man who had acknowledged his problem to his pastor was distributing bulletins to church members one Sunday when his pastor spotted him, jerked the folders from his hands and said, "I don't want you giving AIDS to my people."

The young man scurried out of the building and has never returned. He has wanted to, but has not been able.

They repeatedly asked me, "Why can't the church help us, too? The church has marriage seminars, social action ministries for the poor, prayer for the sick—why can't they help us, too? Why must we be singled out as spiritual incurables?

"Why must we continue to be outcasts?

"Why can't the church move beyond rejection and see us as hurting people who want help just like other sinners?"

I was forced to admit that I really didn't know; maybe it was because of pastors like me who needed to learn that hating sin meant something other than hating sinners.

I needed to experience that move from revulsion to compassion, a compassion that allowed me to reject the sin without rejecting the sinner—to accept the person without embracing his problem. I needed to be reminded and then to remind others that Jesus died for *homosexuals*, was raised from the dead for *homosexuals*, and that his power was available to deliver all sinners from their sins.

Even homosexuals.

CHAPTER SIXTEEN

Becoming Like Jesus

Jerry reapplied to Western Seminary just four months after he went "public" at Hinson.

He had but one year to finish. It had been six-and-a-half years since his withdrawal.

He petitioned the faculty and the administration. He needed permission from several of the administrators before he could reenter school. They all fully accepted him.

Dr. Radmacher asked Jerry to tell his story to the student body; he did.

Jerry's Greek professor offered to help him review his Greek. He told Jerry, "For every hour you're in class, I will privately tutor you for one additional hour."

This he did faithfully.

Jerry finally graduated.

It was a glorious day—a day of celebration that we'll never forget.

He continues to be free.

He continues to serve at Hinson.

He continues to live with the wife who loves him and accepts him and who labors with him to rescue others from homosexuality.

He continues to wait for the day when he might give himself

full time to those who need him so desperately.

He waits patiently, longingly, for a church or a group of churches to move beyond rejection to compassion for a segment of hurting society that needs the great message of deliverance and freedom.

He waits to serve. But he's willing to take all the time necessary to prove that God accepts the unacceptable, heals the hopeless, and rejects only those who reject Him.

It may be that someday the whole church will move beyond rejection to display an attitude toward its hurting like the one expressed in the following letter, written just a few days after Jerry's confession.

> Dear Jerry and Rosie:
>
> We talked for many hours last night after your confession and truthfully tried to examine our feelings. After we got through the initial feelings of unbelief and distaste for the subject of homosexuality, we began to carefully think through it with the Lord's guidance.
>
> We realize that for both of you to decide to honestly confront the church took a tremendous amount of courage and vulnerability.
>
> We stand in awe of the great risk that you took. We wondered how you would feel next Sunday as you walked through the church doors to worship with those same believers and fellowship with many of your friends in your Sunday school class. We also wondered if these believers would handle what you shared with them responsibly and lovingly.
>
> We hope you can know, without a shadow of doubt, that our arms are around you both in a real commitment of unconditional love, to believe the best in you, and to be available to you in any way we possibly can.
>
> Jerry, though you have had victory for over a year, you were careful to point out that you still view yourself as a homosexual, taking victory step by step, day by day. We can't help but feel that we are all not much different in God's eyes.

Aren't we all sinners saved by God's loving and unconditional grace? Aren't we all in the process of becoming like Jesus? Doesn't he promise to present us all perfect and faultless before the throne of God one day?

We both believe that as a body of believers we are to be sharing the hurts, the inconsistencies, and failures of one another. We should be learning daily what it means to be "building up the body of Christ" as he intended.

As Christians we should not excuse or tolerate sin, as you well know, Jerry, but I can't help but wonder where were we when you needed us?

We both feel that your confession was not the only one needed Sunday. We as your friends need to come to you humbly and ask for your forgiveness for not showing you the kind of open, honest love that says "Hey, wherever you're at, it's okay—I love you—I'm not perfect either. You can trust me to believe in you and stand with you."

We are sure that this has been a very hard and oftentimes lonely year for you both. To have the stamina to truly face Satan head-on without the knowledge and support of the body must have been a real struggle.

We hope you can find it in your heart to forgive us for the many times we fellowshiped, talked, and prayed with you and yet missed out on your real need.

We love you and hope that you can feel the heartbeat that both of us share in the writing of this letter.

Appendix

This book was never intended to provide complete clinical or biblical information on the subject of homosexuality. It's just a story—a true story of one man's struggle for deliverance.

Other resource material is available, however. For those seeking information for themselves or others, the following sources have access to books, periodicals, and programs that can be of help to anyone.

Reconciliation
P.O. Box 16751
Portland, Oregon 97216

Love in Action
P.O. Box 2655
San Rafael, CA 94912
(415) 454-0960

A referral list of world-wide Christian ministries to homosexuals may be obtained from:

Exodus International
P.O. Box 2121
San Rafael, CA 94912

The following literature and tapes are available for loan or purchase through Love in Action:

For the Former Homosexual

Tracking the Change Process. What changes should the ex-gay expect? What are some of the obstacles to change?

God Has Spoken. Help in making that firm decision.

What Is Homosexuality? A look at the many sides of homosexuality.

Ex-Gay: Fact, Fraud, or Fiction? Understanding the term *ex-gay*.

The Lordship of Christ. A necessary first step in leaving homosexuality behind.

Advice to Married Men. Insights written by a married man who has overcome his sexual temptations.

Our New Identity. Challenging the term *Christian homosexual*.

Are You Still in the Desert? Our pilgrimage compared with Israel's journey out of Egypt.

Masturbation. A more detailed presentation of this troublesome issue.

Dependent Relationships. Some insights into why gay relationships fail.

Live-In Brochure. An introduction to the Love in Action live-in program.

General Information

The Love in Action Newsletter. Issued monthly free of charge. Especially helpful to those coming from a gay past but equally valuable to those seeking to minister to gays. (Small charge for overseas mailing. Back issues available—write for description sheet and schedule of fees.)

Testimonies. We have testimonies from single ex-gay men, married ex-gay men, single and married ex-lesbians and wives of ex-gay men.

For the Church

Establishing an Outreach to Homosexuals. How a church goes about setting up a ministry.

Establishing Group Meetings. A look at the pitfalls, goals and leadership required in group meetings.

Tips on Ministry. Brief pointers based on personal experiences.

Materials on Child Molestation. A profile of those engaged in pedophilia and advice to parents.

For Friends and Families of Gays

Advice for Parents. The mother of a homosexual gives counsel.

Relinquishment, Letting Go. Vital principles for friends and family members.

What Do You Say to a Gay Christian? An outline of "gay theology" and what your response should be.

My Friend Is Struggling. How to relate to a gay friend.

How To Minister to a Gay Friend. Practical tips on sharing God's love.

How To Pray for a Loved One in Rebellion. A look at Jonah.

Tapes Available

"Frank Worthen's Testimony"
"Root Causes and Prevention of Homosexuality"
"Establishing an Outreach to Homosexuals"
"Pitfalls"
"Help, My Loved One Is Gay!"
"Introduction to Love In Action"

Video Tapes Available (1/2 inch VHS)

"Help for Friends and Families of Gays"
"Emotional Dependency"
"Etiology of Homosexuality"
"Steps Out of Homosexuality"